P
Giving Memo.

"*Giving Memorable Product Demos is the difference between being forgotten and generating raving fans and profits through every word and action.*"
Joel Bauer, Author and Infotainer

"*The authors have given a career's worth of memorable product demos and generously shared their expertise with hundreds of product pitchmen. This book captures all that experience in a concise, valuable, highly-useful text. Giving Memorable Product Demos is a Must Read for every product manager, no matter what your industry.*"
Chris Shipley, Executive Producer, The DEMO Conferences

"*ANY salesperson will profit from this wonderful book. It talks not only about Product Demos but how to put ideas and feelings in the head of the customer to make them want. Great job done Nathan and Claudio!*"
Chris Mulzer, CEO kikidan media, Berlin

"*In all things, your growth is limited by the quality of the experts you choose to learn from. To give powerful and compelling demos, you can do no better than learning from Sennhauser & Gold. This is it; this is the pinnacle. If you don't want to leave your future demos to chance, get this book!*"
Jonathan Altfeld, Trainer of targeted uses of NLP, & author of NLP & Hypnosis home-study programs such as *"Finding Your Irresistible Voice"* and *"The Metaphor Machine."*

"*Finally a book dedicated to the art of giving successful product demos. The advice given by the authors is right on and will make even the most seasoned presenter more effective while planning, preparing, and executing their demo.*"
Kate Purmal, President, Kate Purmal Consulting

"If giving technological demos is important to your business, then 'Giving Memorable Product Demos' is a lifesaver. In it, Nathan and Claudio arm you with all the strategies you need to educate, entertain, and influence your audience, so that they're excited to do business with you."

Mark Levy, Founder of Levy Innovation LLC, and author or co-creator of four books, including *"How to Persuade People Who Don't Want to be Persuaded"*

"This is a bible for all people who think they understand how to demo products. It shows you exactly how to KISS!"

J. Dennis Wolfe, Insurance Broker-Owner and Author

Giving Memorable Product Demos

Demonstrating products with confidence and enthusiasm

Nathan Gold
Claudio Sennhauser

Publisher: Lulu.com

First Edition 2009

International Standard Book Number: 978-0-557-07648-2

Cover by Turgay Uzuncakmak and Felicia Gold

Formatted on a Mac using NeoOffice.
Printed and bound in the United States of America
by Lulu.com
www.Lulu.com
for
The Demo Coach
www.DemoCoach.com

Table of Contents

Appendixes

Preface

This book is about learning how to script and deliver memorable and compelling product demonstrations.

Whether you are in high tech or no tech; whether you are a new kid on the block or a seasoned product demonstrator, this book will provide new insights into delivering more amazing and effective product demos than you have ever given before now.

In every demo, there are two main parts: the content of the demo and the delivery. This book is primarily about the delivery of product demonstrations. The content of your demo should be easy to create once you have learned how to deliver a compelling and memorable demo.

This book is entitled *Giving Memorable Product Demos* because that is exactly what we intend to present in this book. It clearly demonstrates how to use our 7-Step Demo Formula for every type of product demonstration. The techniques described in this book are easily learned in an evening and will surely help you be memorable.

Who is the book for?

This book is for:

- People who have never given a product demo and now have a need to do so.

- People who need to give a product demo, whether it is in person or online.

- Veteran and experienced product demonstrators who want to learn effective new ways to demo their products and services in a more memorable way.

What will you learn?

When reading this book, you will learn:

- How to thoroughly prepare for your demo using our innovative methods.

- A proven, repeatable, and adaptable formula that will make it very easy for you to script and deliver memorable demos.

- Why you need a demo script and how to use it.

- What to do before, during, and after your demo.

- How to deal with nervousness.

When you finish reading this book, you will:

- Feel relaxed and more confident in your demonstration abilities, now that you are armed with our unique Demo Formula.

- Feel assured that your demos will be more compelling and truly memorable.

- Be prepared for just about anything that might happen (good or bad) during a demo.

- Feel a heightened sense of understanding about what a demo is really all about and how to make the most out of each opportunity.

- Know the *Ultimate Secret* to delivering a memorable demo.

- Be able to contact The Demo Coach for a personal and complimentary review of your product demo.

Who are we and why can you learn from us?

We are experts in giving product demonstrations, with over 55 years of combined experience delivering more than 26,500 technology product demos at the time of printing. We have helped hundreds of clients, both large and small, give better demos...resulting in quicker, easier sales, increased media coverage and venture funding, and the earning of many prestigious industry awards.

We are the owners of The Demo Coach company, where we coach demonstrators of all kinds to do things differently leading to more memorable product demos.

We train you to achieve the results you seek, whether it is more product sales, increased web traffic, more coverage in the media, web site referrals, bloggers writing about your product, venture capital, or simply having more personal confidence in front of your audience.

After reviewing thousands of demos (both our own and those of other top demonstrators throughout the world), we defined a simple and flexible formula for giving memorable demonstrations every time. The 7-Step Demo Formula can be learned in 5 minutes and used for a lifetime. It may take you a few hours to work your product or service into our formula, but you will be able to use our proven, repeatable, and flexible formula right away! Our clients have successfully used the Demo Formula to give compelling demos in many different settings, such as venture capital funding meetings, high profile conferences, analysts' meetings, trade-shows, and for the media – with recognition from news outlets such as the *Wall Street Journal* and *San Jose Mercury News* Technology Section.

Our Words of Thanks

A book like this could never have been finished without the help and support of the people around the authors. We both are very thankful for the diligent and thorough editing by Frank Gould, Don Pendell, Claudio's son Morgan, and Nathan's daughter Alaina. They have spent numerous hours making sure the book is in a readable form and logical order and we appreciate their work to no end.

A special thanks goes to Guy Tweedale who was the first person to ever read and edit this book. His comments and suggestions have led us to create a better book overall. We are also extremely grateful for Mark Levy's guidance throughout the creation of this book as he was the one who inspired us to write it in the first place.

Individually, we each have a list of people who have shaped our thoughts and ideas over time:

Nathan:

There have been many teachers and mentors in my life that I have learned from and who I want to thank. However, since I don't want to bore you, I'll make this short and sweet.

The first and foremost "life lessons" teacher and mentor that truly help shape my life begins with my mother. She inspired me over and over again to follow my dreams wherever they take me.

I met my second great teacher at the Masonic Youth Camp in Roundlake, New York when I was 13. Howie Claflin was a camp counselor who taught me more in that summer about being a good person than in all my life. Then, in my first year of SUNY Maritime College, I met Dennis Compton, who had returned to finish his degree. He taught me more about being true to myself than anyone else.

Another huge influence and teacher for me was David Knipfing. I met him in my sophomore year of college. He was 10 years older than me, working in the computer lab, divorced, with 2 children. We spent hours upon hours talking about life and exploring our entrepreneurial dreams. He told me to always seek out opportunities to train and present to people since that skill appeared to be one of my strengths.

One of the most influential people in my career to thank is Bill Fried. He taught me more about people, selling, presenting, and giving demos than everyone put together.

Finally, I want to thank the three most important people in

my life, my wife Leigh Ann and daughters Alaina and Felicia. They continued to stand by me while I followed my dream of writing and publishing a book. Their patience and love is what kept me going year after year.

Claudio:

Over the years I had many tremendous teachers who have helped me become the presenter I am today. My dad, a savvy businessmen in Switzerland, gave me a great head-start as a junior persuader early on. The opportunities to observe and learn from early childhood were endless. My biggest influence early in my career was Rene Seiler, then VP of Marketing at NCR Switzerland. He taught me one of the most important lessons any marketer can learn: "Marketing is Theater!" During my early career, there were countless other teachers in my immediate environment: Paolo Sutter, Albert Scheim, Peter Köppel, and Peter Huber are some of the people who taught me how to influence and persuade with ease and elegance.

Once I moved to the United States, there was no shortage of people from which I learned: Joerg Rothfelder, Joanne Walter, Barry Issberner, Frank Rose, Kate Purmal, and Andrea Butter. Many thanks for sharing and caring!

My list of influential people would not be complete without mentioning Richard Bandler, John La Valle, and Chris Mulzer. They have a knack for cutting rough diamonds into shiny sparkling objects. Thanks for opening my eyes and helping me unlock some powerful resources deep within.

Introduction

The Before and After

Before you read further, it is very important for you to get a benchmark of your demo presentation skills as they are now. For those of you who have never given a demo before, this will be a bit harder. If you feel confident enough to give it a go, record yourself on video giving your first demo without knowing about the Demo Formula. It'll be fun. Go ahead and do it now. Pick a product and record yourself giving a demo for 5-15 minutes. You can use a video camera or a Web cam. It's not going to be published on YouTube, so feel free to keep the camera rolling for one continuous take. It's only for you to see.

We also expect that many people who read this book already give some sort of a demo, and we want you to try something similar.

If you want, it can be your favorite demo, a live event, or just you and the camera. You don't have to rehearse it or write a new script. Whatever is easiest and doesn't take too much time away from you getting to the next chapter.

Go and record yourself now before reading any further.

The real purpose of your demo

You know you need to give a demonstration. And you know you want to do an excellent job. To do so, it helps to think about the real purpose of your demo:

> *The purpose of your demo is to convince*
> *the audience that they should purchase the*
> *product or service you are offering.*

In some cases, you might not be selling directly, but rather increasing awareness of your product. But even this serves to move the sales cycle forward in order to motivate your prospective customer to take some action toward the purchase.

Most demonstrations, from small meeting rooms to large stages, focus on explaining the features of a product. As a result, they turn into an endless show of functions that the product offers, but fail to really address what a demonstration should be about.

Successful demonstrators know this and keep it in mind during the preparation and delivery of their demo, ensuring that it doesn't turn into a mere display of features and functions, but rather a presentation that answers the number one question a prospect has on their mind during the demo:

> *"What benefits will I get from using this*
> *product or service?"*

It cannot be stressed enough that your entire demo must be built around the **benefits** your prospect will get from your product, rather than the **features** your product includes. **Features inform – Benefits compel!**

The ultimate secret of memorable demos

One of the best product demonstrators of our time is Steve Jobs. When Steve Jobs takes the stage, the world's eyes turn to Apple's products. Prospective users are enthusiastically discussing upcoming Apple products months in advance, and they will stand in line for hours and even days, just to be amongst the first users after a release.

This popularity of Apple products is a direct result of Jobs' uncanny talent to transfer his own enthusiasm to his audience.

> ***The most effective way to fully demonstrate your product's benefits is through the transfer of enthusiasm.***

When you successfully transfer your enthusiasm for your product to the people in the audience, they will buy just about anything from you. It's that simple.

Luckily, it is very easy for the aspiring demo pro to watch how Steve Jobs does it – YouTube is full of short highlights of his demos and Apple's own web site hosts a rich archive of his past presentations.

Watch some of his video footage and pay close attention to the emotionally charged words, his intonation patterns, and the body language he uses. He's even got his own trademarked "Boom!" to emphasize cool features; yet another great instrument in his enthusiasm transfer.

Demo at the start of your meeting

A demo is generally a crucial part of every sale. In fact, many people agree that the product demo is the linchpin in a sales cycle. Unfortunately, too many people show the demo at the end of their lengthy company presentations, almost as an after-thought.

Think about it for a moment. When you want to buy a product, you want to see it first, right? What about when you watched your last product demo? Didn't you decide whether or not to do business with that company based largely on the demo?

Keep in mind that the product is the reason that you have been invited to give a presentation.

> *Imagine walking into a car dealership to buy a car and first have to endure a lengthy presentation about the manufacturer, their history, their financial performance, and their competitive positioning...then a detailed PowerPoint presentation about the features of the car, before you're given a chance to sit in the driver's seat or take a test drive!*
> *Talk about a deal-killer!*

Do you honestly think that people really want to hear about who you are and how many investors you have before they decide to do business with you or move to the next step. Highly unlikely!

Many professional sales executives have said that the product demo is the one place in the sales cycle where most sales are ended.

Perhaps a better method would be to do the demo at the start.

Get to the heart of the matter and the reason that you will get money from the person on the other side of the table. Once the demo is over and the audience says, "Wow! That's amazing. Who are some of your customers?" or "Okay. Is your company well funded?"...you'll get your chance to share that information. Most presentations or sales pitches begin by force-feeding the audience with *who, what, when, where, how,* and *why* before the demo starts. Reverse this cycle and do the demo up front. Then, let the questions guide the remainder of your demo and sales call.

Remember, people begin to fall in love with you and your company primarily during and after the product demo.

> ***If you do the demo in the beginning, you get to qualify the prospect earlier on in the sales call.***

Once qualified, you'll either have more time to explore the **real** issues with the customer-to-be – or get to leave early and not waste each other's time. It's a win-win for all.

In addition to being the best approach, a demonstration in the beginning will also make your presentation more memorable because it will set you apart from the competition.

What makes a bad demo?

You have probably seen some really bad demos during your career. Maybe you have even given one, and wish you could take it back.

Here's a short list of things that can add up to a bad demo:

- Arriving late.

- Ending the demo beyond the allotted time.

- Being unprepared.

- Talking instead of demonstrating.

- Acting too confident and assuming.

- Showing feature after feature after feature...

- A lack of understanding about the benefits your prospect is seeking.

- Being sarcastic, argumentative, temperamental, or overbearing.

- Making assumptions about the audience.

Make sure you do not carry any of the characteristics of someone who gives a bad demo. A bad demo will negatively impact the entire sales cycle and message delivery.

People who give monotonous, unenthusiastic demos will be guaranteed a bad grade.

Additionally, try not to make the demo too simple as it may cause the audience to stop paying attention, or worse, feel insulted in their intelligence and experience level.

What makes a great demo?

When you demo your product, each person watching has different and unique needs, concerns, and questions.

If you demo only what you want to show, you may very well miss the essence of your product that people are looking for.

There are many characteristics that will lead to a great demo that shows the actual benefits to your audience and will subsequently move the sales cycle forward. Here are the seven most important aspects of a great demo:

- Having in-depth knowledge of your audience.

- Involving the audience.

- Showcasing your product, rather than talking about it.

- Being logical, concise, and have cohesive information flow.

- Engaging with a meaningful presentation and demo.

- Showing that you have deep expert subject knowledge.

- Giving an enthusiastic delivery.

Okay. Enough introduction. Let's explore the the details of our proven, repeatable, and adaptable 7-Step Demo Formula.

The 7-Step Demo Formula

One of the cornerstones of our training programs and coaching is the ***7-Step Demo Formula***. When you use this formula during the preparation and delivery of your demos, you will notice a huge difference in the response you get from your audiences. They will be more positive and open minded. You will see them lean forward in their chairs and take more interest in what you are about to show them because you have given each person a reason to listen and shown them respect from the moment you walk in.

> ***The Demo Formula has been thoroughly***
> ***tested over many years and in front***
> ***of hundreds of audiences.***
> ***It is proven, repeatable, and adaptable.***

Using the formula will provide you with the outline for giving compelling, powerful, and memorable demos. With these seven steps, you will address almost every situation where you need to give a product demo whether in person or online.

Step 1 - Verify time and introductions

To begin your demo, you should always verify the amount of time you think you have with your audience. You may think you have 45 minutes, but things can change between the time you scheduled the demo and the time you deliver your demo after you've arrived. If you state that you are under the impression that you have 45 minutes, the audience may guide you to take less time or sometimes even more time. In either case, you have shown the audience that you respect their time.

If you are given less time than you expect,
all you need to do is tell the people that you
are prepared to give your demo in that
amount of time.
They will smile and so should you.

Next, let audience members introduce themselves, give their names, and tell what they do for the company. The introductions can be brief or you can take time to ask some good questions from some or all of the attendees.

Recently, we coached a company that was going to their very first venture capital presentation and demo. At the start of their presentation, they confirmed the time. The venture capitalist stopped them and said, "In 25 years of having people come into my office to pitch their products, you are the first one to ever take a moment to verify the time for the demo. Thank you for respecting my time!" Talk about leaving a lasting impression!

Step 2 – Discover, state, or verify business case

In your opening statements following Step 1, one of the most powerful things you can do with your audience is to discover, state, or verify their business case. Even though this may have been covered by the sales or marketing person, you need to show that you understand the business case too.

When you do this, you show the audience that you seek to thoroughly understand their business. You will gain an insight into their specific problems as well as the kind of solution they envision.

If you take the time to let the audience know that you understand their needs, you will stand out among other demonstrators. You will be appealing to your audience's needs, as opposed to your own.

> ***Step 2 is one of the most important steps in the Demo Formula because you are showing your audience that you are not there to waste their time and you understand their business issues.***

Your audience will now know you are there to show them how your product will solve their needs.

If you are not completely sure about their specific requirements, taking the time to **discover** them is a crucial step in your demo. It will help guide you to deliver your demo by showing the audience the features/functions that satisfy what you have just discovered.

If you are absolutely sure about their needs, simply **state** the business case you intend to solve with your product in the demo. Although you may feel confident in stating their needs, you should always **verify** you are correct. One of the easiest ways to do this is to state the business case and follow it by saying something like, "Is that correct and in line with your thinking?"

Step 3 - Provide an outline

By providing an outline, we mean presenting a list of topics you plan to cover and the order in which you expect to deliver them. Although this can be presented visually with a slide, in many cases, a verbal outline of the topics is more appropriate. It is less formal and will also get you to the actual demo quicker.

Your audience needs to know what's coming if they are to follow your demo most effectively.

An outline gives your audience a sense for what you will be covering and it allows them to make room in their brains for the information you plan to provide.

An outline also gives audience members a chance to make sure the topics you plan to cover are well within the scope of what they want covered. You can even give them the opportunity to modify your outline based on their specific needs before the demo begins.

You will be amazed at what you get back from the audience. Sometimes, you will be *spot on*. Other times, they will direct you to the right set of topics for them. Either way, you will find that the audience will be much more receptive to you and your demo after you have asked them for input on what to cover. You can even ask them what order they want topics presented. This will tell you what is most important to them.

Take as much time as you need with these first three steps. However, you can easily combine Steps 1, 2, and 3. For example, you could start out by saying something like, "Thank you for your time this morning. In the next 30 minutes, I am going to show you how my product can help you solve <business issue> by going over X, Y, and Z. Does that meet with your expectations today?"

Step 4 – Make a big statement to position your product

Once you have identified the business case you are proposing to solve with your product, Step 4 is your first chance to make a big statement about your company and product. This is where you give your audience your main value proposition and a sentence or two about your company and how your products will solve their problems.

Step 4 is the place where you set the stage for the rest of the demo.

What you say in Step 4 should raise their eyebrows and give the audience reason to pay close attention to you and even start taking notes.

This step is sometimes difficult or even hard for people who give demos. You can usually get the value proposition statements from the sales and marketing people in your organization. Then, you can tie in the product or service and the needs of the audience to make these statements.

"We make Google a better Google!" "We are the *WebMD* of education." or "Our device is going where no computer has ever gone before." Making big statements like these will cause your audience to position your product properly in their minds.

Step 5 - Show the key benefit first

One of the most powerful things you can do in your demo is to cover the key benefit of your product first. What is the number one benefit your customers get by using your product? Don't talk about it; show it!

Don't make people wait for the best.

When you show the audience how your product can solve their main issue first, you will see a dramatic change in how your audience receives your demo. You will probably even see more interactions between audience members because you have just shown them how to solve their biggest challenge.

Too many people like to save the best for last. This can be problematic because by the end of your demo, several important audience members may have already left the room or their minds are wandering to other things. By leaving the best for last, you risk completely missing the opportunity to convince your audience that your product is exactly what it needs.

Step 6 - Drill down to the finer details

Let's assume you have ten great features and functions that you want to demo and unknowingly to you, the audience is only interested in features 8, 9, and 10. You may lose their attention before you get to the best part of your product that they care about. Or worse yet, you run out of time. You may care about the first seven and your Marketing Department may demand that you cover them. However, if you run the risk of not getting the sale because you were forced to demo in a specific order, what would that prove?

So, how do you know what features and functions of your product to demo? Ask.

All you need to do is talk to a few of the people before the demo begins. Ask them some probing questions about their unique needs and requirements. Then, adjust your demo to cover those immediate needs FIRST! Once you have sold or convinced them in this Step, you may not be required to spend the time to demo the other areas of your product. And, that saves everyone time, including you. You also give the audience the appearance that they are inclusive by allowing them to direct the flow of the demo.

Of course, if there are features of your product that you feel you must show, weave them into the demo as part of the main features they want to see. This way, you are going directly to the core of the unique needs of your new customer to be.

Step 7 - Close with a call to action

Every demo should end clearly, with a call to action. Too often, demonstrators drag on with "just one more feature after one more feature" toward the end of their demo. No audience wants to hear "The last thing I want to show you is..." after seeing a *click-fest* and then having to sit through another four or five feature demonstrations before the demo really ends.

> ### *A well-executed demo always has a clear closing, which includes a call to action.*

You always want to have a reason to follow up or call back.

Being the "technical resource" and the most credible one in the room, you have a unique opportunity to close with a call to action that makes it obvious to the prospect that you will need to contact their technical resource. This contact will give you a chance to debrief from the demo and get information that you may never be able to get through other typical channels. When you follow up, you can even ask specific questions to help you understand how the demo went and how the audience responded after your demo.

Try it. Try setting-up a technical reason for you to call some of the people who attended your demo. You may be surprised how much information you can get being the "technical" one in the group versus the sales or marketing people.

Hint: Audiences are generally more receptive to presenters who demonstrate that they are **not** in a sales role. Product marketing managers often are ideal demonstrators since they spend a great deal of time with the products and (hopefully) also with customers.

> *Non-salespeople are perceived to be more credible and honest. It's a fact of high-tech life. Just accept it.*

To summarize, here are the 7-Steps in the Demo Formula:

1. *Verify time and introductions.*

2. *Discover, state, or verify business case.*

3. *Provide an outline.*

4. *Make a big statement to position your product.*

5. *Show the key benefit first.*

6. *Drill down to the finer features and stories.*

7. *Close with a call to action.*

Follow these steps in your presentations and you will deliver a compelling and memorable demo, which will not only educate your audience about your products or services, but will also get you one step nearer to closing the sale.

Getting Prepared

The more time you put into the preparation of each of your demos, the easier it will be for you to get your message across in a way that will resonate with your audience.

Not only do you need to know your product, its application, and the benefits to your customer, you will need to understand your prospect's requirements fully.

What are their business issues and *problem points*? Why are they looking at your product in the first place and what do they expect it to do? Then, when you prepare the answer to these questions, you will speak the language of your prospective customer and they will feel better about you, too. You will be appreciated as a presenter if you're well prepared. You also demonstrate to your audience that you take your job seriously and won't waste their time.

Know your product

Whenever you demonstrate a product, you're automatically perceived as a subject matter expert. You will need to be able to answer questions about your product that you may not even have intended to show. Too often, presenters believe that by mentioning enough industry specific *buzz words*, they'll be perceived as subject matter experts. Although some members of your audience may appreciate you for knowing some obscure words, the risk is great of losing the majority of your audience.

How do you increase your own knowledge of your product? Use it yourself as much as possible.

You will start to appreciate the most useful features of your product when you use its features and functions on a regular basis. You will be able to share your own experiences in a convincing and competent way. Audiences appreciate a presenter who shares personal stories that highlight the benefits they will enjoy when they use the product.

Also spend some time using your primary competitor's product.

It will give you a real basis of comparison that goes way beyond the understanding you get from merely reading their product's spec sheets, or your Marketing Department's competitive analysis.

When you know your product really well, it gives you the ability to be dynamic and fluid with your delivery. You need to know it inside and out, including shortcuts. You also need to become familiar with the areas of your product that might get you into trouble.

If your product is of a nature which can't be used by yourself alone, such as a business process management system, a complex banking system, or similar product, then talk with some users who are already using your product, both customers and the product developers. Invite them to lunch and find out exactly how they use the product and what features give them the most benefit. If possible, arrange some time to glance over their shoulders while they use the product. The things you learn from your own user base will simply amaze you – the real-life stories you'll collect will be priceless. They will more than make up for the price of lunch.

Know your audience

Your demo needs to be interesting and relevant to your audience. Your customers don't buy your product because of its features, but because of the **benefits** they will enjoy from those features. Only when you really know your audience and their issues will you be able to prepare and deliver a demo that will be interesting and relevant to them.

> *When you deliver your demo in a way that will show tangible benefits instead of features – and answer buyers' needs directly – you are one step closer to success.*

Involve the audience from the first moment by confirming what they want to see.

Ask these types of questions to find out more about your prospect's business:

- What does value really mean to you and your company?

- What does value need to do for you?

- What does value do for you and mean to you in your business?

Know your competition

Knowing your competitive landscape, both present and historic, can give you an edge when giving a demo. Although you should never mention the competition by name, knowing about them in depth can give you direction as to how to demo your product. You never know when someone might be testing you for your knowledge of the competition. Having this knowledge can come in very handy at times.

> *Take the competitor's weaknesses, without mentioning them directly, and emphasize them as your product strengths.*

Frequently, when companies are evaluating products, they will create a matrix of features and functions that they want to see in each product. Although it would be great to get this matrix beforehand, many sales calls do not provide this level of detail. Since you know your products and you should know your competitor's products, you will be able to construct your demo so that your product is the best for that client's needs.

Don't be too obvious with this approach. And, don't ever mention the name of the competition. Phrase it something like: "If you have a concern that a single server will need to accommodate over 2,500 users, our server can handle up to 5,000 today."

Your competition may only be able to handle 1,000 users. Don't be too obvious. We don't want you to become pompous over this. Just loved and admired.

How to demo your best and worst features

Whenever people see your demo, they want to be sure that they see the real product. Many people believe a demo has been prepared, scripted, and rehearsed, and you are only showing the positive sides of your products. Most marketers and salespeople believe you should hide your worst product features.

The key to demonstrating your best and worst features is to remember that no matter what the feature, you need a good story to go with it. It's the stories that people want to hear. It's the stories that people remember. What stories can you tell that people will retell to their office mates, or even better, at their dinner table?

If you remember nothing else from this book, remember this:

> ### *Your compelling and relevant stories are what make you memorable!*

And, being memorable means you have a good chance of being considered in their buying decisions, which, of course, is the ultimate goal.

When you have compelling and emotionally charged stories, people will be more inclined to remember you and your product. It's the stories with purpose and relevance that people love to hear and that help them identify with you and your products.

Now, every product has some feature that could be better. Therefore, you can let your viewer know that there are some features that could be better. When you talk about those features, it is important to mention how your company plans to improve them and how the development groups are working on updates right now.

Of course, if one of your inferior or missing features is one of your competitor's best features and is a customer requirement, you are going to need to map out a strategy for that feature during your demo. You need to have some future plan, statement, or proof that your company is working on this now and will have a better solution very soon. Maybe that solution will even be included in the next release that will be delivered before the prospect finishes the paperwork for the deal. Wouldn't that be perfect timing?

Another very important thing to keep in mind is to be sure that you can identify the benefit that the feature delivers.

> ### *A great feature without any benefit is just a great feature.*

You must be able to demo a feature while telling the benefits of that feature. Keep in mind that feature is a characteristic of a product or service. A benefit is an advantage gained by the buyer. You demonstrate features, but you must consistently link each feature to the appropriate benefit. If you cannot figure out or define what the benefit is for a particular feature or set of features, don't show them.

The 60/30/15/10/5 minute demo

When you are preparing your demo, it is important that you have several versions of the demo. If you prepare for a 60-minute demo, you should also prepare for a shorter version in case the time does not permit you the full hour or you need to reorganize your presentation to satisfy the audience constraints.

We recommend you take your demo that runs for one hour and script it out to run for 30 minutes. Once you have the 30-minute version, we recommend you break it down again into a 15-minute version. Then, knock off another 5 minutes to create a 10-minute version.

You need all of these versions because you may need one of them when the most important person walks into the room late.

They may request that you to give a "quick" version of your demo – to which you can then respond, "Would you like to see the 15 minute or 10 minute version?"

Finally, when you have the 10-minute version ready, you should take one more giant step toward being prepared. Reduce the time of your demo to 5 minutes.

While we understand that 5 minutes is not much time, you may be required to give your demo in that amount of time. It frequently is the case when you go to a conference where you are given a limited amount of time on stage. Or, you may find yourself in a venture capital office one day with 5 minutes to convince the investor to invite you back or to show them more.

The 2-minute demo

Frequently in your career, you will need to be able to give a brief 2-minute demo of your product or service. This is especially true at trade shows where you generally have about that amount of time before you lose the attention of your audience.

You should be able to demo your product in less than 2 minutes, although it may seem impossible at the time.

With enough practice using the following method, you will begin to see the advantage of a 2-minute demo for all of the people involved, including you and your voice.

At a trade show venue, you simply tell your audience that your demo will take 2 minutes. Then it is up to them if they want to see more. This way you briefly qualify the person in less than 2 minutes so that you can be sure to have time for the next person who may be the key executive with whom you most want to meet.

Plus, you have just told the person exactly how much time this demo will take. Keep in mind that time is the most precious commodity people have. Once your audience knows exactly how much time they need to invest in your demo, you will usually see attentive and interested listeners.

If you waste your audience's time by demonstrating feature after feature, no one wins and both parties leave unsatisfied.

Besides, you have wasted everybody's time. But, when you ask your audience in advance of your presentation what's important to them and why, you will be able to focus on the precise points within your demo. For example, should someone ask to see your demo, ask a question like, "What is most important to you about our product?" They may tell you exactly what they are looking for or what their biggest issue is. Then, because you just found out what was most important to them, you can give your 2-minute demo based on their unique needs. By the way, it's a great idea to follow the response to the question above with, "Why is that important to you?" This will give you vital information to direct your demo.

Taking this approach can keep the traffic moving in a trade show, in high-speed networking meetings, and other venues where you have a small amount of time per person. When you get a hot prospect that needs more time, it is best to have a separate area that you can escort them for a full blown demo alone or possibly with another person, such as a technical expert.

Common sense also dictates the need for a 2-minute demo. If you're in a conference or trade show, the person you initially meet may not have more than 2-minutes to watch or they may simply be in the wrong booth. The person behind them could be your next big customer.

> *Anyone is usually willing to give you two minutes. It's those long 15-20 minute demos that will cause the people who are waiting, to leave.*

And, the people watching your demo may be giving you signs that they need to leave too, and NOW!

If you discover that the people you are talking to need a full demo, offer to take them personally to your VIP lounge or other conference room where they can sit down and watch a full demo. People will usually welcome the chance to get off their feet and have a glass of water, tea or coffee. They will also be more apt to remember you for treating them like very important people. If the offer to stop in to the VIP lounge is not appropriate at the time, you can always offer to schedule a follow up with them for after the show.

Practice, practice, practice!

Word on the street is that Steve Jobs prepares and rehearses at least one hour for each minute of a presentation. We find that this is an excellent rule of thumb, especially for those "can't miss," under ten minute demos.

One of the best ways to improve with
practice is to record and listen or video
record and watch yourself, as we did at the
beginning of this book.

When you do, you will see and hear things that no one might tell you about.

Take your practice as seriously
as the demo itself.

Then, after reviewing your own recordings, practice your demo in front of your peers, friends, and family. This will not only give you enough experience to deliver the demo with confidence, it will also expose areas where you will need to fine-tune.

Here are five suggestions to use during your analysis of yourself during playback:

- Watch the complete demo as if you are an audience member. Do not take notes.

- Watch it again and take copious notes about what you see and hear.

- Watch the demo again. But this time, turn your back to the screen and only listen to your voice. Take notes as you listen. What do you hear from yourself? Do you hear enthusiasm?

- Watch the demo again. But this time, turn off the sound. Take notes on what you see yourself doing.

Watch your body language closely. Are you using your facial expressions as a tool to communicate? Pay close attention to any idiosyncrasies or anything else that might distract the audience from your demo.

- One last time, for the fun of it. Back up to the beginning and play it one more time. Only this time, play it at 4x or 8x the usual speed. What you see when you watch yourself in "fast forward" might be fun.

As you watch yourself, answer these questions:

- Do you look and sound believable and credible?

- What are your body language and gestures communicating to the audience?

- How can you improve to make your points even more effective?

- What about the words you use?

- Are they powerful enough and do they convey a high level of enthusiasm?

- What about your voice. Does it register enthusiasm, amusement, and excitement?

Plan for the unexpected

Even though your demo is well rehearsed and you are confident your message is well crafted and in logical order, many things can still go wrong during a demo.

***Experienced demonstrators will have run
into some challenges before, and therefore
know how to work around them,
so they won't become a show-stopper.***

The secret is to always be prepared with a backup plan, just in case. You never know when you might need it.

Have you ever noticed that things that can go wrong will go wrong just at the wrong time? Like having the projector bulb explode in front of 200 people as soon as you are ready to begin. And, it's your projector. Or, having your laptop go into sleep mode while you are explaining a feature of your product. And, when you bring it back, everything is frozen! Or, having your laptop fall onto the floor while you are waiting in the lobby. Of course, it was a total accident. But now the screen is cracked in three places and it won't even start.

What do you do now? What is your backup plan?

***If your demo doesn't have a solid backup
plan, it's like driving a car without
an emergency brake.***

Although we rarely use the emergency brake for an emergency, we always know that there is a backup plan within reach. The same should be true for your product demos.

There are times when you only get one chance to give your demo. In fact, it's most times. If you have a backup plan, you may be able to survive what could be a disaster for you, your team, and the audience should something go awry.

Everyone understands that sometimes things go wrong. Those same people will truly appreciate seeing how you recover when something unplanned happens or a failure occurs.

> ***However, having a backup plan is only
> one side of the coin. The other side is
> you must practice your backup plan.
> Don't just have one.***

As an example, unplug your laptop right in the middle of a practice demo and see what happens. Even if you have a battery in the machine, you may find that your demo gets all messed up when the machine changes from A/C power to battery power. Unless you experiment with some possibilities beforehand, you may be caught off guard. If you cannot recover gracefully, you run the risk of losing the opportunity to give your demo and making the sale.

If you need some help creating a backup plan, start by asking yourself this question: "What are the worst things that can go wrong in my demo?" You should be able to easily come up with a list of answers.

Once you have this list, then answer this question, "What else can go wrong that will ruin my demo?" Make another list.

Using these two lists, map out several backup plans that address the most common or insurmountable possibilities. Most demos will need to have multiple backup plans because of the sheer number of things that can go wrong. Practice those backup plans as often as possible. The more you are prepared, the easier it will be for you to handle any situation that may present itself.

It's true that no one can prepare for every situation that may arise. However, it is good to make sure that you prepare and practice a plan for the most likely and most devastating emergencies. You may find yourself in a situation where you can save the day by being able to recover and continue your demo to its successful conclusion. Being a hero is not such a bad thing for you once in a while, but even heroes have to practice.

The Importance of a Demo Script

There is one ingredient in most demos that is often overlooked and undervalued: The script.

> ***Years of giving demos has proven over and over again that using some form of a script almost always leads to a better and more successful demo.***

Before you skip this chapter, did you know that there are five types of scripts to consider?

- Listing
- Prompts
- Demo Map
- Word for Word
- Hard Plan

You can easily determine which type is appropriate for you based on the venue.

Listing

This is simply a list like any other list you have made in your life. Nothing fancy. Nothing complicated. Just a list of what you plan to present in your demo. It can be on index cards sitting right next to you while you go through your demo. It is an easy reference, used to list out the points you plan to make in your demo.

Prompts

Prompts are a bit more than a list. They include actual words and phrases that you will use to prompt you during the demo. Some people like to start with a listing and add prompts below each item. Although the length of the script will increase, you'll find that prompts will usually be an invaluable aid in helping to remind you of what you wanted to say and do at specific points in your demo. Some people find that prompts are all they need to make sure they say and present all the necessary topics.

Demo Map

This is a very creative and thorough way to script your demo because it will give you a lot of flexibility in how you deliver your demo. Unlike a sequential Listing or Prompts, a Demo Map is a free form diagram of what you plan to do in your demo. One of the advantages to a Demo Map is that it lets you see the entire demo on one page – and be able to move around within the demo script at a glance, given the circumstances of the interactions you are having with your audience during the demo.

A Demo Map is a variation on the theme of the original Mind Mapping techniques developed by Tony Buzan in the late 1960's.

He is an amazingly creative thinker, author, and speaker.

We teach Mind Mapping in our workshops as a recommended way to prepare a demo. The responses we get from people who are not yet familiar with Mind Mapping typically include "why didn't I know about this in college?"

Here is how you create a Demo Map:

Start by taking a blank sheet of paper. In the center of the page, put the name of the demo you will be doing. By starting in the center, it gives you more freedom to spread out in all directions around the center while giving you a complete view of the demo structure you will be creating.

Begin by drawing branches out from the center for each important point to your demo. Write in a word or phrase...or draw a small picture. Add more details for the next level as you expand beyond the center as needed. Move onto the next point in your demo. Do this for everything you plan to present in your demo. Your entire demo should be able to fit on one page. Then, this map can sit right next to you during your demo for easy reference.

To add dimension to your Demo Map, get yourself a set of colored markers. Use color to help you identify parts of the demo that may be related.

You will find several really excellent Mind Mapping software programs available on the web. To see which one we favor, visit our website at www.democoach.com.

Word-for-Word

When you have a specific amount of time for your demo, a word-for-word script will keep you on schedule; otherwise you might run out of time. In most cases, when you have less than 10 minutes to complete your demo, the most effective way to make sure you finish on time is by having a script that you learn word-for-word and click-for-click.

It is not easy for most people to memorize a script and then deliver it in a natural way. In fact, it can be one of the most taxing exercises to put your brain through since your teen years in school.

When you have a specific time limit for your demo...such as when pitching to an investment panel or at a conference...you should hire a coach to take you through the paces. Delivering a word-for-word script requires dedication and the willingness to push through the hard times when the lines don't come naturally. Using a coach for this will ensure that you are prepared when it's your turn to demo.

Hard Plan

Sometimes, the company you are trying to do business with is comparing your products with others in a feature-by-feature comparison. They usually give you a Hard Plan with a predetermined road map of exactly what they want to see and the order they want to see it in as you deliver your demo. This is not very common, but it is a type of script.

In some ways, this may not be fun for you because it could very well limit your style and approach. However, if you don't give the demo according their plan, it will only make your audience confused and even angry, in some cases. Remember, sometimes the people evaluating your product are simply doing what they are asked to do...and conforming to their conventions and needs may make you stand out more positively among the crowd.

We recommend that you give the audience what they want in the order they want it. Then, ask them if you can have a few minutes to show them x, y, and z. When you ask permission to show something rather than taking for granted that they won't mind if you deviate from their script, you show tremendous respect for their time and intelligence.

> ### *The type of script you use is really up to you. Try each one to determine which works best for you and the venue.*

We would not be surprised if you came back and told us that Demo Maps are the only way to go!

One final note about scripting: At a minimum, the script will be very useful to someone who may need to take over, if you become ill or cannot get to the demo on time. Make sure that the other people on your team have a copy of your script, as a contingency plan, just in case. Your script can be a sale-saver, not just for you!

Location Dictates Your Approach

There are four main venues in which demos are typically given: meeting room, online, on stage, and at a trade show. Each of these venues requires a different approach in the preparation and delivery of your demo. A demo that has been designed to be delivered to a small or medium sized audience in a meeting room may not work at all when given on stage to a large audience. A demo that works exquisitely well at trade shows may be totally ineffective during a remote presentation that takes place online.

Meeting room

This is the traditional demo scenario. Your company's representatives are being invited to a client's location to demonstrate your product to the group chartered with evaluating and selecting a new product. Typically the audience for such demos is rather small; they range from one to ten people with diverse functional responsibilities. In a meeting room demo, you will most likely meet some of the people who will ultimately be using your product, members of the management team, representatives from finance and administration, executives who may just drop in for a while, and often an external consultant helping your prospect make the right decisions.

Getting through to all of them is often challenging; you don't want to bore the executives with lengthy technical explanations of how things work, while at the same time giving prospective users enough detail to become excited about how your product will improve productivity and efficiency.

> ***Make sure you know up front who will be attending the meeting and find out their roles within the company.***

If there is an external consultant present, keep in mind that their role may be of understated high strategic importance. They will shine by helping the company find the right product and most likely know your competition's offering in detail. They will be looking for features and functions that set you apart from the competition.

> ***If you are a guest at your prospect's offices, you do not have much control over the infrastructure in most meeting rooms. Bring your own extension cord and a power strip.***

This will ensure that your host doesn't waste valuable meeting time looking for these essential items. If you are demonstrating in a foreign country, make sure you bring along a power adapter designed to work with your host's power outlets.

It is recommend that you always bring along your own projection device. All too often, your client may tell you that they have one you can use. But sometimes you find out their projector may not offer the same screen resolution or format you need. Worse, it may not work properly and require a lengthy configuration to make it function properly with your laptop. This is time better spent mingling with your audience and asking them questions that will allow you to address their real issues.

Sometimes, it's not possible or practical to bring along your own projection device. In those cases, plan for plenty of time before the demo to setup your equipment and coordinate with your contact to make sure you'll have access to the room ten to fifteen minutes prior to the demo. It would be very annoying to your audience – and frustrating to you – if the meeting is supposed to be starting and you're still fine-tuning your laptop and the available projection device.

Online

The number of online demos given each day is rapidly increasing. The reasons for this are simple: they are low cost, very effective, and practical. No need for travel. No need for equipment setup at the meeting site. You don't even have to dress properly.

But, don't let these conveniences fool you into believing an online demo is a *walk in the park*. A true professional will prepare them as diligently as a face-to-face demo in a meeting room. In some respects, you'll even need to prepare more.

> ***Now, as with many things in life, online demos have some inherent limitations with which you will have to deal.***

The worst limitation is that you won't get any visual feedback from your audience – you won't be able to see them and verify that the points you're making are actually getting across. You can't look them in the eyes to see if your enthusiasm for the product is transferring as you intended – unless you are using a video conferencing solution, and even then, it just isn't the same. You will also have to deal with a host of technical challenges, ranging from time delays when sharing your screen remotely...to diminished voice quality and even the possible loss of Internet connection on either side.

However, there are many things you can do to help make the experience more personal and effective for you and your audience on the other side of the connection.

Show yourself

One of the simplest things to do to make the online demo more personal is to add your photo, e-mail, and phone number on the opening screen that is shown through your online connection. If there are more people participating in your online demo from your company, include their pictures, e-mails, and phone numbers, as well! You can even use a webcam, if you want them to really see you. The webcam also gives you the chance to show them something that you can hold up to the camera beside your smiling face!

Pick the right tools

There are many online conferencing and screen sharing tools available. The reliability of these tools is improving rapidly. Many of them allow you to present slides, share your screen, talk in real time, and chat in text windows. Some tools even offer real time polls to engage your audience in the presentation. Whatever tool you use, always use a traditional, telephone-based method to transmit your oral communication. The reason for this is simple: if either of the participating parties loses their Internet connection (which will occasionally happen – Murphy's Law dictates it), you'll still be connected to your audience.

Verify that people can use your online meeting software

When you send out invitations to an online meeting using GoToMeeting, WebEx, or Live Meeting, most people will not take the time to verify that they have everything installed to use it before your meeting starts. You need to ensure that everyone can join. Take the time to contact people a day or two before your demo so that you can make sure they can join your meeting. If you wait until the start of your actual meeting, it could end up taking a lot of unnecessary time helping people get into your meeting. They may need to download a client or install or update something like JAVA, This can also be a problem for some people who don't have Admin privileges on their computers, which won't allow them to install anything!

If at all possible, test your online tools to confirm they will work with Virtual Private Network (VPN) clients and different firewalls. Have someone in the client's office setup a rehearsal to confirm all tools function properly, as you need. You may need to find alternative tools to use in case one tool is unable to connect or operate in different office environments.

Verify what people are seeing

When you use screen-sharing technology in online demos like GoToMeeting and WebEx, the people watching on the other end are usually not seeing things as quickly as you see them. Obviously, the connections to the Internet people use will determine how quickly their screens will be refreshed, which is always slower than your screen. So, there are three simple things you can do to help alleviate the problem of talking about something people are not yet seeing.

1. Have another computer nearby the one you are using for your presentation. Connect to your online meeting just as one of your guests would, except use a wireless rather than a wired connection. It will give you a better representation of what is happening on the audience computers being used for your meeting. Then, glance over at that computer as you change screens to get a better indication of how quickly or slowly the other computers are refreshed.

2. You simply ask the people on the phone if they now see the screen you are seeing. Mention the title of something on the screen that will be easily identifiable. This will surely let you know that your audience is in sync with you.

3. In some situations, it is important to keep in mind to use page down, when necessary, instead of scrolling one line at a time. This action causes large sections of the screen to be refreshed in small pieces, thus increasing the amount of data being transferred between computers. It is also prone to create artifacts and other display distortion that can cause audience confusion and loss of interest. Another point to remember is to share only the windows necessary for your demo and not share clocks or

other windows that create unnecessary data sharing delays.

Minimize the number of PowerPoint slides

Try to minimize the number of PowerPoint slides you use. While many people think PowerPoint is the only way to present their company and products, they will typically bore their audience to tears. If you are giving a product demo, show the product. If you must use PowerPoint slides, try to use a few at the beginning and maybe at the end. And, always end with the opening screen that shows your picture and your contact information.

Use a whiteboard

Many products that allow you to share your screen with other people during an online demo have a whiteboard feature. A whiteboard will allow you to write text and draw pictures during a meeting that can be saved for later reference or meeting notes. Using a whiteboard with your audience can sometimes get them more involved, especially when you turn control over to them to add items to the whiteboard. Think of this as being in a room of people who each take the time to write something on the whiteboard. When the online meeting is over, you might want to send everyone a copy of the notes and drawings made on the whiteboard.

Use a large mouse pointer or a pointing tool

In order to make it easier for remote people to follow your demo, be sure to enlarge your mouse pointer to something larger than you might normally use. And, depending on your software and the colors on the screen, you should choose either a black or white mouse pointer, whichever is easiest to see find and follow on the screen. When choosing colors, make sure you keep in mind there are color deficient (often called "color blind") viewers who have difficulties differentiating between certain colors. The same is true when identifying items on the screen that are color-coded. Use text or shapes on the screen to identify areas of the screen where you want your audience to focus. Don't rely on color alone.

Most screen sharing products have a pointer tool. Rather than just using the mouse pointer, try using one of the built in tools as it will make it easier for people to direct their attention to the area of the screen where you want them to focus.

Instant messaging can be your friend and foe

When you are conducting an online meeting with presenters in different locations around the country or globe, use an instant messenger to send notes and questions back and forth to help guide your demo. Many meeting/sharing applications have instant messenger features built in to prevent the need for an additional application outside the presentation. Just make sure that when you share your screen, you don't share your instant messenger client too. It can be quite embarrassing if your audience sees you texting someone while the demo is in progress. Or, when your friend sends you a message during your demo asking about something that you don't want other people to see!

If you use the instant messaging feature of the screen sharing software, be extra careful when sending messages. It is very easy to send a message out to the whole group watching, which you may not really want to do. You might accidentally say something to the entire group thinking you are sending it to only one person. If this happens, there is little you can do to recover, other than apologizing and hoping your audience has a good sense of humor.

Ask questions

When giving your demo online, you obviously cannot see the faces and body language of the audience on the other side of the connection. So, one of the most important questions you can ask during your demo is, "Are we all on the same page?" This specific question offers people a chance to give you some feedback about how the demo is going at any moment in time. It also gives them the opening to guide you to more important aspects of what they want to see from you.

Use more than one presenter

Another way to keep the online meeting more interesting is to have more than one person deliver the demo. It can be a welcomed change of pace when you have a second or third person on your team give a portion of the demo. Just be sure that you have scripted the parts for each person so you look well coordinated and a little practice time in advance will surely pay off.

Trade show

Trade show demos differ from any other demo type in several ways:

- The visual and auditory distractions around you can be overwhelming, for both you and your audience...whether it's one person or a group of people.

- The number of visitors can be very high during the day. But, always keep in mind that each new visitor is seeing your demo for the first time. This is very important!

- The visitor to your booth will have already been bombarded with a tremendous amount of sights and sounds before even reaching your booth – and after leaving it.

- You must make your demo extremely memorable to ensure that your visitors keep your demo in mind amidst all the other sensory input they receive during the day. You will not have much time to qualify each visitor before your demonstration...and it's easy to mistake a serious product evaluator for an onlooker or hunter for swag.

Work hard at treating every person who is indicating any interest in your product as a serious potential customer. Always keep in mind that each new visitor is seeing your demo for the first time. That is very important! It is better to be cautious and demonstrate your products or services to too many attendees than to risk losing a potential client.

Keep in mind that many people attend trade shows explicitly for the opportunity to watch product demonstrations and talk to subject matter experts.

They may be tired by the time they reach your booth and it is up to you to wake them up and transfer your enthusiasm in a way that will leave a lasting impression well beyond anything else on the exhibition floor.

These recommendations make your trade show demos a success:

Qualify your visitors as quickly as possible

When somebody walks up to your booth and asks if he/she can see a demo of your product, respond by saying "Absolutely. But first, can you tell me a bit about yourself and what you are looking for in a product like ours? This will help me show you the features that are really important to you." This approach allows you to not only gauge how serious the visitor is, but also determine what degree as a prospect. It also demonstrates that you won't be wasting time showing feature after feature and that you are genuinely interested in making the visit to your booth a valuable one.

Keep your energy level high at all times

Giving product demos for hours without a serious break can be very demanding on your body and psychology. Your feet might hurt after a while, your voice may start to show signs of overuse, and your back starts to dream of a nice, relaxing massage. Yet all too often, the most important visitors may show up toward the end of the day and it is critical for you to be in top shape to transfer the enthusiasm you have for your product successfully. So how do you keep your energy level up?

Drink plenty of water
Water will keep your body hydrated and your vocal cords moist.

Bring along small, nutritious snacks
Granola or power bars work well here. Don't eat too many sugary or salty snacks though. Sugar will only give you a short-lived energy boost. Salty snacks will make you thirsty and negatively affect your vocal cords.

Take short breaks
Go outside, if at all possible. A breath of fresh air and natural light will do wonders, especially if you combine them with some light stretching exercises.

Avoid partying late into the night
The temptation to have a really good time in the after hours during trade shows is tremendous. Almost every company organizes special events in the evenings. It may be a great opportunity for you to hang out with your peers. Resist the temptation, though, and your body will thank you the next day. A better plan would be to go for that well deserved massage, a quiet dinner, and then hit the sack early. All too often, trade show workers seem to pride themselves about being able to

put in a hard days work and then party all night. It's a false pride, because nobody really enjoys getting a demo from a low-energy, hung-over person. Even if you may not think the effects of the previous night are being seen, they probably are.

Deal with your bad breath

Fresh breath is essential for people delivering demos at a trade show. Bad breath can ruin a demo before it even begins. So, make Altoids mints (or your favorite breath freshener) your best friend so that your audience will not be subjected to bad breath. In fact, you can even offer one to your audience members as a way to break the ice and invite them to come closer so they can hear you better from the crowds. Most people are happy to take you up on your offer of a free mint or two because they may have bad breath too!

On Stage

Product demonstrations delivered on stage usually require the most preparation. These demos usually take place in front of a sizable audience and may even be recorded or broadcast live for an audience not present in the room.

In many cases, demos on stage may even be a high-profile "can't miss" demo, which require extra rehearsal time.

Many otherwise savvy demonstrators bomb during a stage demo because of the additional pressure and stage fright they may experience.

The best way to combat your fears is to prepare and practice your demo with utmost diligence.

Here are three things you can do to help ensure your success on stage.

1. Script your demo.

2. Have someone else demonstrate the product and you speak the words.

3. Practice. Practice. Practice. Then, practice some more.

Being well scripted and prepared will increase your confidence and allows you to go on stage more relaxed.

Whenever you go on stage to demo your product, you need to consider what the audience is seeing on the screen more than ever. This will ensure people are able to "see" your demo as more than just mouse movements over a complicated screen.

Use Screen Magnification

Many user interfaces use fairly small fonts, which look great when you are sitting in front of the monitor. But, in a large room, even with a very large screen, the text may be too small and too hard to read.

One solution to this depends on the computer you are using. If you are using a PC, try using the magnifying glass to zoom in on a particular area of the screen that you want people to see. The Magnifier does exactly what its title suggests. It's valuable for product demos or almost any kind of presentation.

Here are the specific instructions on how to find and use the magnifier:

In Windows 9*x*, you may have to install this utility from your Windows CD: Insert the CD, click *Start, Settings, Control Panel,* and double-click *Add/Remove Programs.* Click the *Windows Setup* tab, and confirm that *Accessibility* is selected in the *Components* list. Then click *Details,* check the box for *Accessibility Tools,* and click *OK* twice.

To start Magnifier, choose *Start, Programs* (*All Programs* in XP), *Accessories, Accessibility, Magnifier.* If that's inconvenient, just drag the shortcut to a different menu. Or choose *Start, Run,* type magnify, and click *OK.* In most versions of Windows, Magnifier starts by displaying an explanatory message box; check *Do not show this message again,* if you wish.

Click *OK* to start the utility. By default, the Magnifier window appears at the top of your screen, enlarging whatever is under your mouse pointer. If you don't like its size, position the pointer at the edge of the window and drag to make it larger or smaller. Reposition the magnifier by placing the pointer inside the window and dragging it to any screen edge. Alternatively, you can make it a free-floating window in the screen's center.

The Magnifier dialog box lets you set the magnification level, decide whether the magnifier should always show what's under the pointer, determine whether it should follow text cursors as you type and edit, and a few other things. Try using the defaults at first. They are especially handy if you want to show others in a large room what you are doing with the mouse or what text you are typing. On the other hand, if your goal is to enlarge a single hard-to-see part of the screen (such as a toolbar with tiny buttons), uncheck *Follow keyboard focus* and *Follow text editing*. Then make sure the area you want shown is in the magnification window, and press **Alt-M** to turn off *Follow mouse cursor*. Click *OK* to minimize the dialog box (in Windows 9*x*) or click the minimize button (in other versions).

Naturally, you don't want to be messing around with the Magnifier settings during the demo. If your keyboard has a <Windows> key, you may be in luck with a shortcut! For example, pressing **Windows-Up Arrow** will increase the zoom level, and pressing **Windows-Down Arrow** will decrease it.

If you are using a MAC, there is a very nice zoom feature whereby you can simply hit a set of keys and the screen will zoom into the area where the mouse is hovering.

Hold down the Control key, then drag TWO fingers up your Mac's trackpad. Whoah, right? This reveals the secrets of controlling the trackpad gesture zoom.

We close this chapter with one of the most helpful secrets to know for giving on stage demos. We have learned this from stage actors.

How to avoid dry mouth

When you go out on stage to give a demo, you may be a little more nervous than usual, especially when you have bright lights staring you in the face. You might even have cameras too! This environment can immediately lead to a dry mouth.

Before stage actors go out on stage, they take some

Vaseline® Petroleum Jelly and lightly coat the outside of their teeth on the top and bottom. When you do this, your lips will not stick to your teeth, there is no taste, and it will absolutely prevent an embarrassing situation for you if your mouth suddenly dries out. Also, keep a glass of water handy where you are sitting or standing.

Dealing with Nervousness

"According to most studies, people's number one fear in life is public speaking. Number two is death. Death is number two. Does this seem right? This means to the average person, if you have to go to a funeral, you're better off in the casket than doing the eulogy." - Jerry Seinfeld

Surveys report 70 to 75 percent of the adult population fear public speaking – this includes giving product demonstrations. Even experienced public speakers often experience public speaking anxiety. Successful individuals and top-notch speakers like the evangelist Billy Graham, former president Ronald Reagan, and Chrysler's former CEO Lee Iacocca have publicly expressed their fears when getting up and speaking in front of an audience.

There are many names for this fear of public speaking, including speech fright, speech anxiety, stage fright, public speaking anxiety, and communication apprehension. We simply call it nervousness.

Uncontrolled nervousness can make the life of a product demonstrator miserable and limit the potential of success.

Luckily, the fear of public speaking can be effectively managed.

People with communication apprehension often feel anxious only

67

in specific settings. These include public speaking, meetings, group discussions, and one-to-one conversations. Public speaking is the number one fear associated with communication apprehension. It's also the one that most affects a product demonstrator.

A major factor that leads to communication apprehension is self-talk.

Self-talk is thinking about your performance – and its chance for success or failure – that goes through your mind before and during a demo. Negative self-talk that focuses on potential failure increases anxiety. It stems from fear.

For most people, it's uncomfortable to be the center of attention for an extended period of time. When speaking in public, all eyes are on you. It's easy to fall into a pattern of negative self-talk as a result of it. For a professional product demonstrator, negative self-talk should not be too much of an issue. Instead delve into the demo within the first one or two minutes to divert the attention of your audience to the screen or your product. When you present your demo like a pro at the beginning of your meeting, you will not have to endure a long period of time as the center of attention.

The fear of failure is most likely the biggest contributor to nervousness during a demo.

This is not the fear that your demo will totally bomb, but rather how your audience will react to your demo and if it will meet their expectations. People whose anxiety rises from fear of failure tend to view pubic speaking from a performance perspective. They see themselves performing in front of an extremely critical audience just looking for the presenter to make a mistake.

Demonstrators with this perspective feel they must create a perfect demo and deliver it flawlessly. To alleviate the fear of failure, understand that the audience is on your side. Your audience is there to get information about your product and see how it will benefit them - they are absolutely not there to rate your demo performance. Having a loose script with just a few bullet points will help you to focus on communicating, rather than performing. Knowing that your demo has been practiced thoroughly will also help you feel confident. Your key points, major messages, jokes, and examples have been tested with your co-workers, family, and friends.

Another major cause of communication apprehension is that too many of us have simply learned to be fearful of public speaking.

The fear of public speaking has been modeled and reinforced. The good news is that any learned behavior can be unlearned.

So how do you reduce this learned anxiety?

Here a few things you can do to deal with nervousness:

Breathe from your diaphragm

Take a moment to take inventory of your normal breathing pattern. Are your shoulders moving with each breath? If so, you are exhibiting shallow breathing. You don't fill all of your lungs with air, just the top half. This means that some of your internal muscles are tightened and do not allow enough air to fill all of your lungs. This increases anxiety in a significant way!

This way of breathing is also unnatural. We are all born to

breathe from the abdomen – just watch a baby breathing and you will see its belly move, rather than its chest – but some of us have learned to breathe unnaturally from the chest. After years or decades of this, it even feels natural to breathe from the chest, but it is not. It's easy to retrain yourself to take deep, full breaths to start breathing naturally again. Simply focus on your breathing and inhale so that your abdomen is moving in and out with each breath.

Sigh

Take a deep breath and sigh while you breathe out. Sighing is a natural way to decrease inner tension and this is a great way to alleviate your anxiety just before you start your demo.

Progressively relax your muscles

This technique was developed in the 1930s and is still one of the most effective ways to decrease tension and lower anxiety. It consists of systematically tensing and relaxing each of your fifteen muscle groups. The fifteen muscle groups are: hands, biceps and triceps, shoulders, neck, lips, tongue, mouth, eyes and forehead, abdomen, back, midsection, thighs, stomach, calves, feet, and toes. Start at the top with your forehead and eyes, and work your way down, tensing each group twice for about 10 seconds before relaxing it. This technique will require some practice, but once you get the hang of it, you'll be very relaxed by the time you reach your toes. It is recommended to set aside a few minutes each day to practice this technique. Perform this in the minutes before your demo and you will notice a measurable decrease in your communication anxiety.

Visualize

Many athletes and top performers already use visualizing to their advantage by performing their activities with success only in their head. Since this works very well for top performers in any field, it will also work for you. Use the power of your mind's eye to your advantage when preparing your demo to reduce communication apprehension successfully.

There are two ways to visualize. The first is to associate yourself into the moment completely. This is where you will see what you expect to see when you present your demo. This is the first person view and it allows you to give a demo in your mind's eye as if you were giving the demo in real life. The other way of visualization is to envision yourself presenting in front of an audience from a bird's eye point of view. See yourself giving the demo as if you were watching yourself from the outside. Both of these two techniques will lead to astonishing results.

Before your next demo, run through it in all of its details in your mind's eye – first as if you were looking at yourself from an observer's point of view. See yourself smile and having a good time while you enthusiastically deliver the demo of your life. Once you have completed this step, switch to a first person's view and deliver the demo in its entirety.

For another exercise using visualization, the next time you're lying in bed getting ready to go to sleep, visualize yourself giving the demo. It will help you on the day of the demo!

Use music

Music is an amazing way to deal with communication apprehension and nervousness. When you use music that inspires and motivates you, it will help you to listen to that music before your demo. When the original Rocky film came out, it had an amazingly motivating soundtrack played to the scene when Rocky ran up the stairs in Philadelphia at the end of his training phase just before the fight. Find some music that works for you and let it automatically calm you down and excite you when needed.

Smile

Many people forget to smile during a demo. However, smiling can be a way to help your nerves calm down too. And, a smile will convey a better message to your audience than a frown or no smile at all. Try smiling the next time you feel nervous. You should automatically feel better, calmer and in control of your emotions.

Moments Before the Demo

Arrive really early

Arriving early can make the difference between a successful demo and one that goes down in flames. By arriving at least 30 minutes early, you'll have a chance to get situated and comfortable, long before the meeting and demo is scheduled...even if you start in the lobby. It also gives you lots of time so you can hopefully deal with any delays in arriving at the location of the demo.

You never know what can go wrong **before** you arrive, not to mention the things that could go wrong **after** you arrive.

Giving yourself a 30-minute early arrival window will calm your nerves.

This gives you the time to focus on the truly important thing: delivering a memorable demo.

Another huge reason for arriving really early is that you may get the chance to speak to some of the people coming to your demo. When you catch people before your demo starts, you get the opportunity to make friends and ask some questions.

Making friends with the people and asking some questions beforehand will usually lead to a much more intimate setting for you because now you know some people in the room. You may even discover some information that will help you personalize your demo a bit and make it more enticing to your attendees.

Set up your kit and test everything

After you arrive early, take the time to set up your kit and test everything to be sure there are no problems. Even though your computer looks like it started up properly, be sure and check to see that everything you expect to use is operating correctly.

One of the biggest challenges people have in setting up is counting on an Internet connection in the room where the demo is being held. You cannot count on this.

You need to make sure that your demo can stand on its own without relying on the people you are visiting to provide you with things like Internet access.

You should even bring your own extension cord because some rooms you meet in will not have a conveniently located plug.

Mingle with the audience before the demo begins

This will give you a chance to find out the mood of the people. It will also let you ask some questions. The answers may help you during the demo. Some key questions that tend to elicit responses geared toward your demo are:

- "What do you hope to see here today in the demo?"
- "How's the mood around here today?"
- "Do you have anything specific you'd like me to cover

today in the demo?"

Asking questions is one of the most effective ways for you to generate rapport with your audience, especially if you are sincere and really listen to the answers.

Sometimes, there is no time to mingle before the demo.

> ***Feel free to ask some questions at the beginning of your demo because it connects you with the audience and they will appreciate the time you give them to talk about their needs.***

It also gives you time to verify information you think you already know.

Here are more suggestions for questions:

Verify or find out who will be attending the demo

When you know who is coming to see your demo, it will be easier for you to know how to conduct your demo and what to cover. Each person will be coming with his or her own agenda. However, if you know who will be attending your demo beforehand, you will be able to adjust your presentation accordingly. Be flexible and accommodating at all times.

Ask both business and personal questions, if appropriate

When you mix up the questions you ask people, it lets them know that you are not just there for business, but that you care about them as a person. When you ask about non-business related things in a person's life, that person will naturally become more open to hearing what you have to say and show. It's almost like they owe you the time because you befriended them.

"What's most important to you about...?"

When you ask this question, it typically elicits information that tells you what's most important to the listener. After asking this question, it's good to follow with "Why is that important to you?" Asking this question combo several times can give you lots of information about the people to whom you present. Try it out and see what you learn from your audience.

These questions, along with other specific ones on your personal list of favorites, do not have to be asked before or even at the beginning of the demo. They can be asked anytime and they can also be directed at specific features and functions in your demo.

How to Get Rapport and Keep It

There are dozens of techniques for achieving and maintaining audience rapport. Below, are some of the techniques to use when giving a demo. They will help you when building rapport with your demo audience whether it is one person or a crowd of thousands.

Ask good questions as the demo progresses

Ask questions, but not too many. Too many questions makes you appear like you have not done your homework or that you really do not understand their business. Be sure to ask your questions sincerely. And, most importantly, listen to the answer without interrupting the person speaking.

Also, take the time to think about the answer before you fire back. By consistently pausing before you answer, it gives you a chance to think through the words in the question before you answer without considering the breath of the question. Sometimes, when you answer a question from the audience too quickly, you give the appearance of being pompous and so confident that you cannot be asked anything that you cannot answer. Once in a while, we even recommend that you pause a second or two to think, then say, "I'm not real sure about that. May I get back to you later today or tomorrow on that one?"

Not having the answer to a question can easily be the reason to get back together with information that was important to your prospect. It also gives you the chance to move the sales cycle forward.

Try asking this question and see what happens: "What keeps you up at night?"

When you ask this question, be prepared for a variety of answers. The answers will probably surprise you. In most cases, people will tell you something about their business. In some cases, people will relay some personal information. It's a really interesting question because you get some really great information about some of the most important things in their business. You may even find that some of that information you discover can be integrated into your memorable demo, on the spot!

If you want, you can change the question to, "In regards to your business, what keeps you up at night?" In either case, you have their attention!

Here are some additional questions that can help build rapport with the people in your demo:

"Are there any specific features or questions that you have about our product before I begin? If so, then I can make sure to address those during the demo."

This question can be risky because they may ask you to demo something that you have not tested or worked with in the past. However, if you want to add a little risk to your demos, this question can offer you some very interesting diversions from your normal demo scripts. You may certainly choose to omit this question from your routine.

While this question might open you up to anything, it is also an opportunity to show the people in the room that you are willing to take a risk. It also shows them that you are a flexible demonstrator and willing to ask them what's important to them. This builds rapport with any audience so long as it doesn't backfire and cause a huge debate among the audience members.

...and a few more questions you can ask: "What do the people around here spend most of their time thinking about?" or "What is the biggest unsolved challenge in your business these days?" or simply, "What do you think?"

Check in with your audience

By occasionally asking your audience if you are on the right track with the demo, you give them the chance to help define what is most important to them.

> *By asking this question at certain points in your demo, you can be sure that you are giving them what they want and need.*

If not, they should feel comfortable asking you to switch it up and change directions.

Also, asking this question gives you a chance to get some reaction from the audience, which is hopefully a nodding yes!

Make eye contact with the audience

You'd be amazed at how little people will make eye contact sometimes.

Some people will not trust you if you don't make eye contact, at least once in awhile.

Make sure you look each audience member in the eye as you pan the room and be sure to include everyone, at least once. It's a simple thing to do, but it takes practice if you are not comfortable with it.

How to Begin Your Demo

Okay. You are all prepared. You have your script. You have practiced many times and consider yourself ready to deliver the demo.

There are five things you can do as you begin your demo that will immediately change how the audience perceives you and how they will feel about your demo. Try these out and see how people react positively before you show your first feature:

1. Verify the amount of time you have to demo

It's your turn to take the floor and give your demo. How do you start?

When **YOU** go into a demo to watch someone present, what is one of the first questions on *your* mind?

Isn't that question "I wonder how long this is going to take?" You may not ask it out loud, but don't you typically want to know how much time it is going to take? It's no different with your demo.

So, there are several things to consider regarding the timing of your demo:

- The first is to verify that the amount of time you *think* you have is still the amount of time you'll actually have. Many unexpected things come up between the time you schedule your demo and the time you deliver your demo. So, when you verify the time you think you have, you immediately show the audience that you respect their time. You also give them the chance to tell you that the original timing for the demo is still okay or that it needs to be adjusted.

- Once you know how much time you'll actually have for your demo, adjust your demo to meet any time changes. That's why it is so important for you to know how to present your demo in less time than you think you have. And, remember if you end up having less time, that doesn't mean that you should merely speed up your pace of speech so you can cover the same material in a shorter period of time. Your audience needs to have time to absorb what you say...and rushing through doesn't allow this important time.

- As you know by now, you should be prepared for any length demo. However, if you typically give a demo that lasts for 45 minutes and the decision maker tells you that they only have 30 minutes, you need to adjust or you run the risk of causing problems. Having asked what's important to the decision makers also helps you adjust to the salient points of your presentation.

Here are a few examples to get you started:

- "Thank you Ed. Before we begin, I want to verify the time you have set for this meeting. It is my understanding that we have 30 minutes. Is that still the case?"

- "Thank you Sarah, for that great introduction. In the next 20 minutes, I want to take you on a tour of..."

- "I'd like to begin my brief 15-minute presentation with you today by covering three topics."

Each of these statements gives the audience a clear picture of how much time they need to devote to your demo. Once they have this in their minds, they'll be more relaxed and be open to what you have to say. Of course, then it is up to you to give them your memorable demo using the techniques described in this book.

2. Introductions

After covering the amount of time you have for the demo, introductions are in order. Once you have established the timeline, have everyone introduce herself and himself. Then make sure you get everyone's name correctly. Unless you can memorize the names after hearing them once, write them down.

You can use the time during the introductions to even ask a few questions. The answers to those questions might help you determine a better approach to your demo. What if you discover that one of the most important things on their minds about your product is X and you've planned for Y? Wouldn't it be better to know this before the demo rather than during or after?

3. Assure your audience the demo is not generic

Next, most people despise canned demos. They never say it, but they do. So, why start off on a negative when you can turn it around to an instantly positive feeling for everyone in the room. All you need to do is ask the audience if they would mind if you did NOT do a canned demo.

When you ask this question, watch the audience member's reactions. You will probably notice that they become more friendly and approachable because you have just alleviated a big fear and concern. People do not want canned demos. They want a personalized demo just for them and their business concerns.

In an ideal world, you use your own product. This will not only increase the familiarity you have with the product, but will also give you lots of real life examples you can then share with your audience.

If that's the case, it'll be easier for you to proclaim: "Rather than waste your time, let me show you what I do with this product to get *my* work done."

4. Assure the audience that you know who they are

This is a subtle but important point that needs to be conveyed to your audience. If you don't know who is in your audience, how can you direct your presentation and demo to meet their concerns and needs. If you show that you know something about the audience and their business, they will usually be more open to you as a presenter.

One way to be sure to address this is, just before your start your demo, take a few minutes to summarize and present what you know about the audience and their business, especially their immediate concerns. If you have done your prep work and homework, a few sentences about the company will let the audience know that you understand them.

5. Let the audience know that you know your subject inside and out

Audiences want to know that they are getting a product demo from someone who really knows the product inside and out. Have you ever received a demo from a person who is obviously new to the product and is trying to make believe he or she really knows their product?

Everyone needs to cut his or her teeth on a new product or feature set in public. However, you still must practice these demos many times to build your authority and gain the credibility you need to make a big sale.

How are people to know that you know your product inside and out? Start by telling them how long you have been using the product. Then, make sure they can see a level of enthusiasm for your product that compares to no one else.

What to Do During the Demo

Be engaging with a meaningful presentation

John Medina is a developmental molecular biologist and research consultant. He is an affiliate Professor of Bioengineering at the University of Washington School of Medicine. He also is the director of the Brain Center for Applied Learning Research at Seattle Pacific University. In short, John knows a thing or two about how the brain works. In his book *Brain Rules,* he outlines his discoveries about the human brain. Two of them are especially relevant to every demonstrator:

> ***First, the brain has a tendency to tune out after 10 minutes. And second, it ignores subjects without contextual meaning.***

Medina began teaching in 1993 and since then, he has asked all of his students the following question: "Given a class of medium interest...not too boring and not too exciting...when do you start glancing at the clock, wondering when the class will be over?" The answer consistently has been 10 minutes. According to Medina, peer-reviewed studies confirm his observation. Medina writes, "Before the first quarter hour is over in a typical presentation, people usually have checked out."

Knowing this 10-minute rule is highly important for any product demonstrator.

> *If you want to hold your audience's*
> *attention throughout your entire demo,*
> *you need to build in an attention getter*
> *shortly before each 10-minute segment.*

This doesn't have to be anything too drastic – an interesting and relevant story might do the trick. Engage your audience with a question at that point is also a great way to keep them from drifting off. If you are presenting online, you can use a quick poll to give your audience a chance to participate actively.

The second insight about the brain ignoring subjects without contextual meaning comes directly from our evolutionary history, according to Medina. In an interview with *Business Week* in July 2008, he explained, "We didn't care about the number of vertical lines in the teeth of the saber toothed tiger. We cared about whether it was going to clamp down on our thigh. We were more interested in the meaning of the mouth than the details."

Let's assume you demo a document management system that lets users do redactions – blacking-out parts of information for security and privacy purposes. The first thing you might do is to show some statistics and facts about identity theft. Point out just how much of a danger it is to have important information visible to the world.

__After the audience has been given a reason to care, you can delve into the details of the system and they will likely pay a lot more attention than if you merely presented the technical details without the context.__

Another way to engage contextually is to let the audience actually touch and try the product (if possible). People remember things they have sensually **experienced** much more than if they just **see** them.

Think back in your own life. What was the first computer you ever used? Chances are, you remember the exact brand and circumstances around your first moments with a computer. What is the first car you ever drove? Chances are, you remember not only the make and model, but even the color of the vehicle.

__There is some magic behind letting people experience your product first hand – make that magic work for you.__

Especially if you present a new, revolutionary type of product, people will not as easily forget it if they have had a chance to try it out themselves.

Give an enthusiastic delivery

Transferring enthusiasm is really THE key to delivering a compelling and memorable demo. You need to have a lot of enthusiasm to be able to transfer it successfully. If you're not really all that excited yourself about your product, then you can't really expect other people get that excited.

Spend time thinking about the most appropriate and powerful words that help describe your product in a persuasive way.

Take a moment to listen to some of Steve Jobs' demos and notice the words he uses. He has a very rich vocabulary and typically describes his products and how he's using them with carefully chosen words that convey his enthusiasm in a big way.

Use some secret tools to simplify your demos

Some people cannot type very well or they may have trouble spelling. This can be quite embarrassing for you and your team during a demo.

Take the time to get familiar with some simple tools that make you look better and make your demos run more smoothly.

We suggest you check out Quick Type and ActiveWords as tools that save you time typing and automatically correct your spelling errors. Also, take a look at Yuuguu to replace your screen sharing software. There is no client to download as they provide a way for people to see your screen using only a browser. As always, check to make sure people can join your meeting before the day of your meeting.

What if some audience members are online and others are in the presentation room with you?

The answer is simple. Give your demo as if everyone is online. By definition, you will need to go slower for the information and screens to reach every part of the world, just as if you were doing an online-only demo.

Repeat all questions

This is a pet peeve of some people, especially those who cannot hear the questions asked of you, by others.

> *Be sure to repeat <u>all</u> questions that are*
> *asked so that everyone can be sure*
> *they heard the question.*

It's amazing how many presenters neglect to do this, only to risk the chance of losing some or all of the audience while they go off answering a question that not everyone heard in the first place.

"Here is my most important point"

There are many times during a demo when the audience's attention will wander. No matter how exciting and riveting your product demo, there are bound to be dips in the audience's attention span. This is natural and should be expected.

> *When you say slowly and clearly, "Here is*
> *my most important point," you will get*
> *everyone's attention in an instant because*
> *the audience knows that the next thing they*
> *are about to hear is "important."*

They will always sit up and take a deep breath when they hear these words.

Following this, it is up to you to present your best information with power and emotional appeal. What you say following the words "Here is my most important point" may just be the only thing they remember!

The 3 most effective words you can use

I don't know.

That's right. "I don't know," are some of the most effective and powerful words you can use in any product demo.

> ***By not having the answer to every single question, you demonstrate humility that actually serves to build more credibility with your audience because you are willing to admit you don't know. You show that you are just like the audience.***

And, humility is a good thing in building relationships with people you want as your clients. This advice is not to take away from your enthusiasm or knowledge of your product or service. As the person giving the demo, you are perceived as the subject matter expert until you prove yourself otherwise. It is more about humility and showing respect for the person watching the demo.

Of course, if you don't have the answers to too many questions, it will call your expertise into judgment by your audience. That is not a good thing. Having to say, "I don't know." more than twice in a demo probably means you need to learn more about your product or service. On the other hand, no one really likes a know-it-all, especially the type of people who want you to know that they know everything about everything. The motto of these people is typically, "People who think they know everything are particularly annoying to those of us who do."

It is unwise to make up answers on the fly just because you want to be perceived as an expert. Sooner or later your audience will discover that you gave them a conjured up answer, and you will be humiliated.

> *Making up answers for the sake of*
> *having an answer to a question*
> *will sacrifice your credibility.*

Another important reason is, it gives you a perfect reason to get back in contact with someone who has seen your demo when you don't have an immediate answer to a question. After you get back to them and report your findings, it gives you a unique opportunity to learn more, like, how the audience responded to the demo...or if there were any other questions you could answer for them...or something else you can do for them. You always want a legitimate reason for following up...and not knowing the answer to a technical question is a great one. As an example, "I don't know, Betty. I will find out and get back to you in the morning."

> *Successful marketers are always looking*
> *for legitimate reasons to communicate with*
> *their audience because they know that each*
> *reason gives them another opportunity to*
> *pass along more benefits about their*
> *product or service.*

What about questions during a demo?

The most important aspect to questions during a demo is to let the audience know when they can ask questions. However, you should let them know this at the beginning of the demo.

If you want to encourage questions during the demo, say so up front. If you want to have attendees hold their questions until the end or until some specified break, say so up front. If you don't have time for questions at all, say so up front.

During a recent demo, the presenter was asked a question about 10 minutes into the demo. They responded by not answering the question and asking the audience to hold all questions until the end.

That was a bad move. The person who asked the question stopped paying attention for the rest of the demo because he felt scolded like a 7 year old in school. When this happens, you not only lose the spontaneity of questions, many of the people in your audience may then feel like questions are unwelcome!

Let people know up front what the plan for Q&A is going to be. If you want them to hold their questions for later, suggest that they quickly jot them down so they won't forget them when the time comes. This approach shows your concern and invites them to participate with questions.

Some people say that the sale doesn't start until the first question. It shows that the person watching your demo is now curious about something they saw or heard. It shows interest.

Remember this when responding to questions:

> ***Never respond to questions with statements like, "That's a great question" or "That's a really good question." These responses really do sound obnoxious and they tell the rest of the audience that they better ask great and really good questions of you.***

This response will sometimes shut down people from asking questions because they become fearful (subconsciously) of not asking a "great" or "really good" question.

The better way to respond to a question, is to start with phrases like, "Thanks for asking that question," "I appreciate your asking that question," or "Thanks for reminding me about that!"

And, when you don't know the answer or you want to fake not knowing, start with something like: "Hmmmm...I'm not really sure of the answer to that question. So, let me make a note and find out for you after we're finished here. Okay?"

Then, be sure you get back to them in a timely manner. People will judge you on how rapidly and thoroughly you follow-up.

Take notes

Take notes during your demos, especially the questions people ask. It shows respect for the person asking the question. By taking notes on all of the questions you hear, it will be easier to report back as to what happened in the demo.

> ***Taking notes will help you and others prepare for future demos.***

The answers to those questions can help train peers in what to expect when they give their demo.

Those notes can also help you structure your demos so that some of the questions are eliminated. In other cases, you may just want a particular question asked at a specific time. It can be a wonderful thing when someone asks you a question that you have heard a hundred times before, but it comes at the perfect time. So, you smile, thank them, and smoothly move onto the next part of your presentation.

Your notes may also come in handy when the product team needs input on how to improve the product. Questions about your product can often lead to fantastic new features. Once those features are implemented, the question may be a thing of the past.

Finish on time or even early

If you want to have a better chance at leaving a good and lasting impression on your audience, finish your demo on time. If you finish late or run over the amount of time you have been given, you will steadily lose the rapport you have built up during the demo. If you make people late to their next meeting, they will remember you for making them late.

Another interesting and unique approach that will definitely keep people talking about you and your demo is to finish early.

> ***When you finish your demo with ten minutes to spare, you give everyone a chance to reflect on what they just saw and it gives people a chance to get to their next meeting with less stress.***

The conclusion of your product demo is as important as the opening. Just as every great symphony has an opening, a body, and a conclusion, so must your demo.

To let the audience know that you are finished, you can begin your concluding remarks with words like "Finally," "In conclusion," or "To conclude this demo."

Be sure to finish on an upbeat tone. This is your last chance to leave an emotional mark on your audience. If you conclude with poise and purpose, they just may be convinced to do business with you.

What to Do After the Demo

While you are still in the meeting room following the demo, first ask if there are any more questions. Next, take time to ask the audience or specific people what they thought. "What do you think?" or "How do you think the demo went today?" are fair questions to ask. You are bound to get some insight into how you just did and you may even get feedback that can help you in your next demo.

> ***You can also be brave and ask people where you can improve your presentation.***

This question can disarm your audience and they may be very honest by giving you information to help lead you to giving better and more powerful demos in your future.

With your team

The best time to get feedback on your demo from your team is immediately after the demo when it is fresh in everyone's mind. Take a few minutes to debrief each other. It can only lead to making you a better demonstrator.

***Very soon after you leave the demo venue
with your team, ask some hard questions
and take the time to improve for
the next demo.***

Here are some questions you can ask yourself and your team:

- Who will follow up with the unanswered questions?

- What did we do right?

- What did we do wrong?

- What can we do to improve the demo the next time?

- How can we be more memorable next time?

- How could we have been better prepared?

- What additional questions should we have asked before, during, and after the demo?

- What questions came from the audience that might help direct a better product?

We recommend you put these questions in a simple questionnaire that you fill out after each demo.

Your demo and first impressions

One of the best ways to improve your demo skills is to continually practice on new people to get their first impressions. New, fresh eyes, force you to go back to the beginning and will remind you of areas of your product that may need specific emphasis or de-emphasis. It's also a good reminder because we frequently become accustomed to and automatic in our demos that we assume the audience knows everything that we know about our products and/or services.

Working with people who have never seen your demo before will also lead you to experience the "first impression" experience that will help cement the steps you need to take in each of your demos.

> ***Have you ever wished you could have***
> ***another chance at a first impression?***
> ***Now, you can!***

Every time you give your product demo to new people, you are creating that important first impression. Whatever they see you do and show will be the impression that stays with them for a long time. Be prepared and go for it! You only get one chance to make a first impression, right?

Most people spend a majority of their time learning what to say about the specific features and functions of their products. You may be surprised to find out that you are spending too much time and emphasis on what to say.

Speaking of what to say, Dr. Albert Merhabian is a professor at UCLA who published a quantitative and qualitative study on the process of communication between people. He divided the process of communication into three main areas: words, voice, and facial expressions. Today, most people interpret facial expressions in this study as body language.

According to this study, only 7% of a message is communicated with words or "what you say." Your voice accounts for 38% and your body language makes up the rest at 55%.

Can you believe this?

Can you believe that 93% of communication is NOT based on WHAT you say, but HOW you say it and the way you sound?

If you believe these findings, the way to develop your talent is to work on HOW you deliver your demos.

Would you believe that people who have poor speaking voices, the kind that set your teeth on edge, are almost always unaware of how it affects people? We are our most enchanted listeners and it's human nature for each of us to believe that nobody speaks as well as we do.

So, how's your voice? Do people ever say anything about it, good, bad, or indifferent? Maybe you can even get some voice lessons. Most colleges have Speech departments or Speech Therapists can help you. They get to practice their art and you get to learn something about how to use your voice more effectively.

One last thing...

By now, you have learned everything from us that you need to do and think about as you prepare to deliver your next demo. We hope you have enjoyed the way we put this information together for you.

However, this is only the beginning. Each demo you give should be a learning experience for you, which leads you to continually get better and better. Now, you need to take what you have learned and turn it into practice and real situations.

All right. Do you remember the "before" video recording we asked you to make in the beginning of the book? Did you do it? Hopefully, you did because now you can have some real fun.

After you reformat your demo to make use of The Demo Formula, record yourself again and then compare the result with the recording you made before reading this book. Go ahead and do this now. Do this for yourself. You deserve it.

May the sun always shine on your face and may the wind be at your back! Go forth and start giving more compelling and memorable demos now. It will be more fun for you and even more fun for your audiences. They will hopefully remember and talk about you for a long time.

Appendixes

Appendix 1:
Hints, Tips, & Tricks

Use an optimized PC or Laptop

You should try to use a laptop that is fairly high powered, so that it reduces latency between activities in your demonstration. Additionally, even the best hardware will falter if you are running too much on your system. Prior to the demonstration, you should reboot and open only those applications you need to use for the demo.

Buy as much RAM as you can afford

Frequently, a computer will start acting slower than it is, simply because it does not have enough memory.

Use a fast hard disk; at least 7200 rpm

A lot of laptops come with 5400 drives, to reduce heat and increase battery life. However, disk drives are noticeably a bottleneck in the speed of any computer, and therefore a faster internal drive is highly recommended.

Defragment your hard disk often

On Windows, frequent defragmentation is essential to making sure your machine functions quickly. However, on Mac OS X (all versions) and all versions of Linux, defragmentation is not typically necessary.

On a laptop, set it to 'maximize performance' not 'maximize battery life'

On Windows, go to Power Options Properties and set the power scheme to "Presentation". This mode will never turn off your monitor or hard disk, and the system will not go into standby or hibernation.

On a Mac, go to the Energy panel in your System Preferences. On most Linux systems, power management can be configured using either Gnome Power Manager or KDE Power Assistant.

Ensuring that your screen doesn't go into standby is important: many projection devices will automatically go into a sleep mode themselves when they do not receive an input signal. Waking these projectors up, can take away valuable time from your demo.

An uncluttered desktop

Even if it means temporarily dragging superfluous icons into a different folder, having a clean desktop minimizes distractions and increases how professional your demo appears.

Typing Assistant

A typing assistant is an invaluable tool to use during a software demo. Our favorite is QuickPhrase, a handy tool where you can store your snippets of text used during your demo and add them to your application in a snap. This avoids the risk for awkward typos.

PowerPoint 'B' and 'W' key

Although we would prefer that you did not use PowerPoint slides in your demo, there are times when you might want to make the screen go blank. Turning the projector off is one option, but that takes time to power down and power up again. Blocking the bulb with a book is an option too, but it is not a very classy way to interact with your audience.

There is a little known secret in PowerPoint that you can use, which will sometimes impress the audience so much that they will ask you how you did that.

When using PowerPoint in Slide Show mode, you can hit the B key on your keyboard and the screen will go Black. Hit the B key again, and the slide will come back to life.

If you prefer to be in the spotlight, you can hit the W key and the screen will go White. This is especially useful if you are in a dark room and a great way to do hand waving and shadow animals. As with the B key, when you hit the W key again, the screen turns from white to the last slide that was showing.

Batteries and bulbs

Invariably, when you use battery operated devices such as pointers, clickers, mobile phones, and PDA's, the battery will quit right in your demo. Worse, it may not even allow you to turn on the device.

If you use any battery operated or battery backup devices in your demo, be sure and bring extra batteries. If you use a projector, be sure and have a back up bulb. It can mean the difference between success and failure.

Appendix 2:
Basic Presentation Skills

A successful demonstrator needs to master the basic communication techniques. In addition to the medium of speech, non-verbal communication is always used to support the spoken word. The skillful communicator deliberately uses such means as facial expression, loudness of voice, tone of voice, and gestures to support the spoken word. It is therefore imperative that the successful demonstrator masters the techniques of effective communication.

The following factors should be considered by any presenter to demonstrate to a group of people (what comes out of your mouth):

Audibility

Audibility is a matter of having enough force to be heard. If you are talking to a small group gathered around your desk you will naturally need less volume than if you must be heard by people in the last row of an auditorium.

Through experience, learn to adjust your voice to the appropriate level for each occasion. There are two extremes, of course: too loud and too soft. A person who speaks too loudly can be very irritating, and cause discomfort to the listener. On the other hand, someone who speaks too softly (often a sign of shyness) cannot communicate effectively.

Articulation

Speaking loud enough is not much good if the words cannot be distinguished. Good articulation demands that the final voiced consonant of each word be pronounced. In addition to improving articulation, pronouncing the final consonants clearly will advantageously slow down the rate of speech.

Modulation

A monotonous, dull speech pattern will take the life out of the most interesting topic. Modulation is varying your voice pitch up and down. It is the music of your voice. Never be ashamed or too shy to let your voice register enthusiasm, amusement, or excitement. After all, modulation is the single most important aspect in your ability to convey enthusiasm – and transfer it to your audience.

Rate of speech

In presenting a product, the normal rate of speech is between 120-140 words per minute. To really keep the audience on the edge of their seat, bump the rate up enough to be a little bit different. We suggest the correct rate of speech should be between 130 and 150 words per minute. Having said that, it is important to stress that varying your rate of delivery can be very effective. Excitement is usually registered by an increase in speed of speaking: Slowing down the rate of speech can be used to put emphasis on an important point.

Volume

Although audibility and volume are related, it is important to realize that volume, like modulation, should be varied. It is better to lower your voice if you wish to stress a point. If you are talking to a group who are disorderly and inattentive, you are usually most effective by lowering your voice than to shout to overcome the noise.

Voice stressing

The meaning of your verbal communication can be altered by the stress put on certain words and even syllables. Try putting stress on different words or phrases in the following sentence:

"You are the best" - clearly indicates that *you* is the most important word in this sentence.

"You *are* the best" - indicates that you *are* (as opposed to are not) the best "of" or "at" the topic being discussed.

"You are the *best"* - obviously makes it clear that you are the *best* at whatever the topic of the discussion is.

By changing the emphasis on different words in this sentence, you change the meaning of the sentence significantly...along with the actual "feeling" your audience gets from your delivery of the sentence.

Tone

How many times have you heard the statement, "It's not what he says, but how he says it?" It is particularly important for presenters to keep their tone from portraying impatience, irritation, boredom, or intolerance. Always maintain a tone that conveys positive emotions such as enthusiasm, interest, and helpfulness.

Appendix 3:
Recommended Reading

Below, is an alphabetical listing of recommended books and resources to help you give memorable product demos and presentations.

- *5 Steps To Professional Presence: How to Project Confidence, Competence, and Credibility at Work* by Susan Bixler

- *11 Steps to Powerful Public Speaking* by Jacki Rose

- *45 Second Presentation That Will Change Your Life* by Don Failla

- *Accidental Genius* by Mark Levy

- *Artful Persuasion: How to Command Attention, Change Minds, and Influence People* by Harry A. Mills

- *Awaken the Giant Within* by Anthony Robbins

- *Better Than Bullet Points: Creating Engaging e-Learning with PowerPoint* by Jane Bozarth

- *Beyond Bullet Points: Using Microsoft® Office PowerPoint 2007 to Create Presentations That Inform, Motivate, and Inspire* by Cliff Atkinson

- *Brain Rules: 12 Principles for Surviving and Thriving at Work, Home, and School* by John Medina

- *Clear and to the Point: 8 Psychological Principles for Compelling PowerPoint Presentations* by Stephen M. Kosslyn

- *Death By PowerPoint* by Michael Flocker

- *Death by PowerPoint: How to Avoid Killing Your Presentation and Sucking the Life Out of Your Audience, Your Effective Tip-Kit for the Effective Use of PowerPoint* by Cherie Kerr

- *E-mail Selling Techniques (That Really Work!)* by Stephan Schiffman

- *Finding Your Irresistible Voice,* CD-Set by Jonathan Altfeld

- *FOR SALES SAKE MEDITATE!* by Vincent J. Daczynski

- *Getting To Yes: Negotiating Agreement Without Giving In* by Bruce M. Patton, William L. Ury and Roger Fisher

- *Go for No!* by Richard Fenton

- *How to Make Sales Forever* by Jeffrey Gitomer

- *How To Master the Art of Selling* by Tom Hopkins

- *How to persuade people who don't want to be persuaded* by Joel Bauer and Mark Levy

- *How to prepare, stage, and deliver winning presentations* by Thomas Leech

- *How to Run Seminars and Workshops: Presentation Skills for Consultants, Trainers, and Teachers* by Robert L. Jolles

- *How to Win Friends and Influence People* by Dale Carnegie

- *How to Wow with PowerPoint* by Richard Harrington and Scott Rekdal

- *How to Write and Deliver a Winning Speech* by Darren Lacroix

- *Idea Mapping: How to Access Your Hidden Brain Power, Learn Faster, Remember More, and Achieve Success in Business* by Jamie Nast

- *Influence: The Psychology of Persuasion* by Robert Cialdini

- *Influencer: The Power to Change Anything* by Kerry Patterson

- *Jump Start Your Book Sales: A Money-Making Guide for Authors, Independent Publishers and Small Presses* by Marilyn Ross and Tom Ross

- *Knockout Presentations: How to Deliver Your Message with Power, Punch, and Pizzazz* by Diane DiResta

- *Language for Learning - Presentation Book D* by Siegfried Engelmann and Jean Osborn

- *Lessons in Mastery* by Anthony Robbins

- *Life Is a Series of Presentations: Eight Ways to Inspire, Inform, and Influence Anyone, Anywhere, Anytime* by Tony Jeary

- *Little Green Book of Getting Your Way How to Speak, Write, Present, Persuade, Influence, and Sell Your Point of View to Others* by Jeffrey Gitomer

- *Little Red Book of Selling* by Jeffrey Gitomer

- *Live with Passion! : Stategies for Creating a Compelling Future* by Anthony Robbins

- *Magic for Dummies* by David Pogue

- *Mark Wilson's Complete Course in Magic* by Mark Wilson
- *Mind Mapping: Kickstart Your Creativity and Transform Your Life* by Tony Buzan
- *Mind Maps at Work: How to Be the Best at Your Job and Still Have Time to Play* by Tony Buzan
- *Never Cold Call Again: Achieve Sales Greatness Without Cold Calling* by Frank J. Rumbauskas Jr.
- *New Sales Speak: The 9 Biggest Sales Presentation Mistakes and How To Avoid Them* by Terri L. Sjodin
- *Persuasion* by Jane Austen
- *Persuasion Engineering* by Richard Bandler and John LaValle
- *Persuasion, Negotiation, and Influence Skills* by Brian Tracy
- *PowerPoints!: How to Design and Deliver Presentations That Sizzle and Sell* by Harry Mills
- *Power Presentations: How to Connect with Your Audience and Sell Your Ideas* by Marjorie Brody and Shawn Kent
- *Power, Influence, and Persuasion: Sell Your Ideas and Make Things Happen* by Harvard Business Essentials
- *PowerPoint Advanced Presentation Techniques* by Faithe Wempen
- *PowerPoint Magic* by Pamela Lewis
- *Presentation Skills For Managers* by Jennifer Rotondo
- *Presentation Zen: Simple Ideas on Presentation Design and Delivery (Voices That Matter)* by Garr Reynolds

- *Presentations and Public Speaking* by SparkNotes Editors
- *Presentations for Dummies* by Malcolm Kushner
- *Presentations Plus* by David A. Peoples
- *Presentations that Change Minds: Strategies to Persuade, Convince, and Get Results* by Josh Gordon
- *Presentations: proven techniques for creating presentations that get results* by Daria Price Bowman
- *Presenting to Win: The Art of Telling Your Story* by Jerry Weissman
- *Principle Centered Leadership* by Stephen Covey
- *Real Leaders Don't Do PowerPoint: How to Sell Yourself and Your Ideas* by Christopher Witt
- *Sales Presentation Techniques: That Really Work* by Stephan Schiffman
- *Sales Questions That Close Every Deal: 1000 Field-Tested Questions to Increase Your Profits* by Gerhard Gschwandtner
- *Say it With Presentations, Revised & Expanded: How to Design and Deliver successful Business Presentations* by Greg Zelazny
- *Secrets of Closing the Sale* by Zig Ziglar
- *Secrets of Question-Based Selling: How the Most Powerful Tool in Business Can Double Your Sales Results* by Thomas Freese
- *Selling 101 : What Every Successful Sales Professional Needs to Know* by Zig Ziglar
- *Selling: Powerful new strategies for sales success* by Gary May

- *slide:ology: The Art and Science of Creating Great Presentations* by Nancy Duarte

- *Speak Like a CEO* by Suzanne Bates

- *Strategic Selling* by Robert B. Miller, Stephen E. Heiman, Tad Tuleja, and J.W. Marriott

- *The 7 Habits of Highly Effective People* by Stephen Covey

- *The 12.5 Principles of Sales Greatness* by Jeffrey Gitomer

- *The 25 Sales Habits of Highly Successful Salespeople* by Stephan Schiffman

- *The 45 Second Presentation That Will Change Your Life* by Don Failla

- *The Art of Woo Using Strategic Persuasion to Sell Your Ideas* by G. Richard Shell and Mario Moussa

- *The Back of the Napkin: Solving Problems and Selling Ideas with Pictures* by Dan Roam

- *The Best Damn Sales Book Ever: 16 Rock-Solid Rules for Achieving Sales Success!* by Warren Greshes

- *The Big Book of Presentation Games: Wake-Em-Up Tricks, Icebreakers, and Other Fun Stuff* by John Newstrom and Edward Scannell

- *The Confident Speaker: Best Your Nerves and Communicate at Your Best in Any Situation* by Harrison Monarth

- *The Craft of Scientific Presentations: Critical Steps to Succeed and Critical Errors to Avoid* by Michael Alley

- *The Elements of Style* by E.B. White

- *The Exceptional Presenter: A Proven Formula To Open Up and Own the Room* by Timothy J. Koegel

- *The Magic of Rapport* by Jerry Richardson

- *The Magic of Believing* by Claude Bristol

- *The Magic Power or Emotional Appeal* by Roy Garn

- *The Mind Map Book: How to Use Radiant Thinking to Maximize Your Brain's Untapped Potential* by Tony Buzan and Barry Buzan

- *The One Minute Manager* by Kenneth H. Blanchard and Spencer Johnson

- *The One Minute Manager* by Spencer Johnson

- *The Overnight Guide To Public Speaking* by Ed Wohlmuth

- *The PowerPoint Detox: Reinvent Your Slides and Add Power to Your Presentation* by Patrick Forsyth

- *The Presentation Skills Workshop: Helping people create and deliver great presentations* by Sherron Bienvenu

- *The Quick and Easy Way to Effective Speaking* by Dorothy Carnegie

- *The Sales Bible: The Ultimate Sales Resource* by Jeffrey Gitomer

- *The Sales Success Handbook: 20 Lessons to Open and Close Sales Now* by Linda Richardson

- *The Science of Influence: How to Get Anyone to Say "Yes" in 8 Minutes or Less!* by Kevin Hogan

- *The Ultimate Sales Machine Turbocharge Your Business with Relentless Focus on 12 Key Strategies* by Chet Holmes

- *The Workplace Skills Presentation Guide* by Laurie Cope Grand

- *Think and Grow Rich* by Napoleon Hill

- *Toastmasters International Guide to Successful Speaking: Overcoming Your Fears, Winning Over Your Audience, Building Your Business and Career* by Jeff Slutsky, Michael Aun and Toastmasters International

- *Unlimited Power : The New Science Of Personal Achievement* by Anthony Robbins

- *Use Both Sides of Your Brain: New Mind-Mapping Techniques* by Tony Buzan

- *Visual Thinking: Tools for Mapping Your Ideas* by Nancy Margulies and Christine Valenza

- *Walk the Talk…and Get the Results You Want* by Eric Harvey and Al Lucia

- *What's Your Point?* by Bob Boylan

- *Winning Presentation in a Day: Get It Done Right, Get It Done Fast!* by Rhonda Abrams

- *Words that Change Minds: Mastering the Language of Influence* by Shelle Rose Charvet

24862111R00074

Made in the USA
Lexington, KY
08 August 2013